FORMS *for* HELPING
Children
with OCD

FORMS *for* HELPING
Children
with OCD

E. Katia Moritz, Ph.D.

Childswork ChildsPLAY

Secaucus, New Jersey

©1998 Childswork/Childsplay, LLC, a subsidiary of Genesis Direct, Inc., 100 Plaza Drive, Secaucus, NJ 07094. 1-800-962-1141. All rights reserved.

Printed in the United States of America
8 7 6 5 4 3 2 1

ISBN # to come

Contents

Contents *(continued)*

Introduction

Obsessive-Compulsive Disorder (OCD) is a complex condition. Its symptoms are varied and range from mild to intense. OCD requires the therapist to have special knowledge and skills to implement an effective treatment program.

Children and adults experience similar OCD symptoms. Even though more studies have been conducted in the adult population than the pediatric population, the research shows that the most effective treatment modalities for OCD are behavior therapy and psychopharmacological treatments.

The behavioral treatment of OCD requires a high level of compliance, motivation, and commitment on the part of the patient. Treating childhood OCD is an even greater challenge than treating adult OCD. The therapist must know how to adapt the behavioral treatment to a child. The treatment must be more fun, more childlike, and more hands-on. Emphasizing education about the illness and the treatment is important for both the parents and the child. Their understanding of OCD and the rationale behind the behavioral exercises helps increase the effectiveness of the treatment.

The literature on treating childhood OCD is limited. This book attempts to provide simple and practical clinical tools to help therapists who treat children with OCD. The forms in this book emphasize education, assessment, and behavioral strategies. There is little background information about the disorder. Prior knowledge and treatment experience in OCD is assumed. The forms are easy to use, can be adapted to individual needs, and can be photocopied from the book for use in treatment.

The assessment tools included in this book were designed to facilitate information gathering in a clinical setting. Their validity and reliability in clinical settings have not yet been established.

Intake Session

Gathering information and documenting it is an important part of treatment. The "Intake Session" form was developed to help the therapist collect information relevant to treating childhood OCD. This form was not designed to collect all the information needed for therapy (e.g., consent forms, insurance information, etc.). It should be used as a supplement to other forms the therapist already uses in practice. Some of the questions in the "Intake Session" form may not pertain to the treatment directly but may be important to help conceptualize the diagnosis (e.g., OCD in the family, onset after streptococci infections, etc.).

Intake Session

Child's Name: _____ Child's Age: _____

Date: _____ Child's DOB: _____

Present in Session: ( ) Patient ( ) Mother ( ) Father ( ) Others _____

Background Information

Parent's marital status:　　( ) married　　( ) divorced　　( ) other

List of children and adults living with the child (including ages):

Name of School: Grade:

Type of classes child attends:

Description of Problem

Current symptoms:

Past symptoms:

Age of onset: Diagnosed by:

Medications

Prescribing physician's name:

Phone number: ( )

Have parent's signed consent to contact the above doctor: **( ) Yes ( ) No**

Intake Session *(continued)*

Medications *(continued)*

Current medication: _____ , _____ mg.

_____ , _____ mg.

_____ , _____ mg.

Side effects:

Symptom Impact on Current Functioning

	None	Mild	Moderate	Severe
School				
Home				
Social				
Personal Care				

Co-morbid conditions:

Prenatal/Developmental History

Difficulties during pregnancy:

Full Term: **( ) Yes   ( ) No**

Type of Delivery:

Medical History

Health problems:

History of head trauma: **( ) Yes ( ) No**

History of Streptococci infections: **( ) Yes ( ) No**

Intake Session *(continued)*

Family History

Evidence of OCD or related disorders in parents or siblings?
If so, describe:

Other mental illnesses in family:

Parental participation in the symptoms:

Parental understanding about the illness:

Summary of the Case

Recommendations:

Provisional diagnosis:

Rule out:

Short-term/long-term goals:

Session Notes

OCD can present itself in a large variety of symptoms. In order for behavioral treatment to be effective, the therapist must know when and how a symptom was addressed and the child's responses to the interventions. This form was designed to help the therapist organize and document information gathered during the sessions. Accurate session notes will provide the therapist with an important tool for measuring clinical progress and directing the treatment.

Session Notes

Child's Name: _____ **Child's Age:** _____

Present in Session: ( ) Patient ( ) Mother ( ) Father ( ) Others _____

Session summary:

Symptoms addressed:

Behavioral observations:

Short-term goals:

Homework assignments:

Other observations:

Weekly Checklist for Parents

The accurate reporting by parents of a child's behaviors between sessions is an important part of a successful treatment. The form "Weekly Checklist for Parents" was designed to facilitate for parents the process of reporting their child's progress and therefore help the therapist adjust the treatment accordingly. Treatment gains that generalize to other aspects of the child's life are also noted on this form.

Weekly Checklist for Parents

Child's Name: _____   **Week Ending:** _____

Child's Age: _____

Directions (to parents): Please fill out this form and return it to your child's therapist before the next session. Answer the following questions based on your child's behaviors between the sessions.

1. Changes in your child's symptoms this week:

Positive	0	1	2	3	4	5	6	7	8	9	10
	none										*extreme*

Negative	0	1	2	3	4	5	6	7	8	9	10
	none										*extreme*

Comments:

2. General changes in the child's mood or behavior:

Positive	0	1	2	3	4	5	6	7	8	9	10
	none										*extreme*

Negative	0	1	2	3	4	5	6	7	8	9	10
	none										*extreme*

Comments:

3. Child engaged in daily activity that he or she was unable to engage in before:

	0	1	2	3	4	5	6	7	8	9	10
	less										*more*

Comments:

Weekly Checklist for Parents *(continued)*

4. Estimated time spent having obsessive thoughts:

0	1	2	3	4	5	6	7	8	9	10

average number of hours daily

Comments:

5. Estimated time performing compulsions:

0	1	2	3	4	5	6	7	8	9	10

average number of hours daily

Comments:

6. Child motivated to resist symptoms:

0	1	2	3	4	5	6	7	8	9	10

none   *extreme*

Comments:

7. Child able to resist symptoms:

0	1	2	3	4	5	6	7	8	9	10

none   *extreme*

Comments:

Weekly Checklist for Parents *(continued)*

8. This week's behavioral homework assignment:

completed successfully	avoided	N/A

Suggestions:

9. Parents able to refrain from helping child with OCD symptoms including giving reassurance:

0   1   2   3   4   5   6   7   8   9   10

less   *more*

Examples:

10. Child's understanding of the symptoms:

0   1   2   3   4   5   6   7   8   9   10

less   *more*

Comments:

11. Significant incidents this week:

Positive	Negative	N/A

Describe:

Other relevant information:

Activities Affected by Symptoms

This checklist is designed to help the therapist assess which areas of normal functioning are affected by the symptoms. This form has not yet been validated and only assesses the most common activities that may be affected by OCD. The "Activities Affected by Symptoms" form should also help assess the areas that need to be targeted during the behavioral treatment program.

Activities Affected by Symptoms

Name: _____ **Age:** _____ **Date:** _____

Directions: Put an X next to the items that the OCD (habits and thoughts) makes it hard for you to do.

___ Taking a bath or a shower	___ Washing my hands or my face
___ Brushing my teeth	___ Brushing or combing my hair
___ Getting dressed	___ Taking my clothes off
___ Going to the bathroom at home	___ Going to a public bathroom
___ Wiping after using the toilet	___ Touching garbage bags
___ Hugging my parents	___ Touching my friend's hand
___ Touching other kids' belongings	___ Petting a cute animal
___ Touching dirty dishes	___ Touching raw food
___ Tying my shoelaces	___ Touching door knobs
___ Visiting hospitals	___ Being close to someone with a cold
___ Going through doorways	___ Playing with my friends
___ Walking	___ Mailing letters
___ Throwing things away	___ Cleaning and organizing my room
___ Making my bed	___ Reading
___ Writing	___ Doing schoolwork
___ Talking to people	___ Making decisions
___ Eating	___ Using staircases
___ Doing math	___ Traveling by bus, train, or car
___ Moving my body	___ Stop thinking the same thought

Other activities that OCD interferes with:

Common Obsessions

Children often have difficulty discussing their obsessive thoughts. They may feel embarrassed or feel frightened to talk about these thoughts. This checklist was designed to help the therapist assess which obsessive thoughts should be targeted for behavioral treatment.

Common Obsessions

Name: _____ **Age:** _____ **Date:** _____

Directions: Put an X next to the thoughts that come into your mind and cannot be quieted, the thoughts that you think over and over and that make you very nervous. At the bottom of the page write down any thoughts that repeat in your head or make you scared that are not already listed below.

___ Something bad is going to happen to someone I love if I don't do a certain behavior.
___ I am getting sick.
___ I am going to wish something bad on someone.
___ I am going to get contaminated by others' germs.
___ I am going to vomit.
___ I am going to get dirty.
___ I may write or say a curse word when I don't want to.
___ I am going to hurt someone.
___ I am going to get a tummy ache.
___ I am going to say something wrong.
___ Someone is going to hurt me.
___ I have to know exactly where all my stuff is.
___ My mom or dad is going to get sick.
___ Dirt is everywhere.
List other thoughts that repeat in your head:
List thoughts that make you scared:

Urges and Compulsions Checklist

Compulsions, very often referred to by children as "habits", are the most common expressions of OCD. They are the most overt of the OCD symptoms and an important target symptom for treatment. This checklist contains the most commonly seen compulsions.

NOTE: This is not a comprehensive list of all OCD compulsions. The therapist must also assess for compulsions that are not included on this form.

Urges and Compulsions Checklist

Name: _____ **Age:** _____ **Date:** _____

Directions: Put an X next to the behaviors that you feel you have to do in order to feel less nervous.

___ Rewrite what I already wrote.	___ Read the same things over and over.
___ Touch the floor.	___ Touch objects.
___ Touch my body.	___ Hurt my skin.
___ Ask questions over and over.	___ Wash my hands a lot.
___ Retract steps.	___ Arrange objects in a certain order.
___ Make things look even.	___ Switch lights on and off.
___ Lock doors.	___ Check faucets.
___ Check electrical appliances.	___ Smell things.
___ Count over and over.	___ Review conversations.
___ Make lists.	___ Confess.
___ Pick my nose a lot.	___ Blink.
___ Tap my foot.	___ Fake a cough.
___ Make noises.	___ Spit.
___ Pull my hair.	___ Pick my scabs.

List any other "habits" that you have:

Building a Symptom Hierarchy

This form was designed to help you organize the OCD symptoms in a hierarchical order. Some symptoms are harder to deal with than others. In these forms the child places the symptoms on each mountain slope in order, from easier to harder. Targeting the easiest symptoms first (the Beginner Slope) will increase the likelihood of the child being able to accomplish all therapeutic goals.

Building a Symptom Hierarchy

Name: _____ **Age:** _____ **Date:** _____

Directions: The slopes are divided into five degrees of difficulty:

The Beginner Slope. This is the easiest of the trails. You can stop with very little effort. It's not that scary.

Advanced Beginner Slope. A little harder, but still OK. You have to put a little more effort into stopping.

Intermediate Slope. This slope requires more effort. It is now harder to stop or control.

Advanced Intermediate Slope. Difficult. This is a very difficult trail, very hard to stop.

Expert Slope. This is the most difficult slope and is almost impossible to stop on.

Using the lists of obsessions and compulsions from the forms Activities Affected by Symptoms, p. 19, Common Obsessions, p. 21, and Urges and Compulsions Checklist, p. 23, fill in the spaces next to each type of slope. Include even the ones that bother you only a little and are easy to stop (Beginner Slope).

Slopes	Obsessions & Complusions
Beginner Slope:	1. 2. 3.

25

Building a Symptom Hierarchy *(continued)*

Slopes	Obsessions & Complusions
Advanced Beginner Slope:	1. 2. 3.
Intermediate Slope:	1. 2. 3.
Advanced Intermediate Slope:	1. 2. 3.
Expert Slope:	1. 2. 3.

Targeting the Symptoms

Having the child participate in establishing treatment goals helps increase treatment compliance. Together, the therapist and child can outline the behavioral program using the "Targeting the Symptoms" form. In order to organize the symptoms in this form, use the list of symptoms from the "Building A Symptom Hierarchy" form on page 25.

This form utilizes an analogy: the degrees of difficulty in skiing and the effort involved in mastering a new skill. A successful behavioral program involves creating progressive and realistic goals for the child as well as involving the child in organizing the targeted symptoms. Like the "Building a Symptom Hierarchy", this form is divided into the Beginner Slope, Advanced Beginner Slope, Intermediate Slope, Advanced Intermediate Slope, and Expert Slope. Use the Beginner Slope form first and, as symptoms improve, move on to the next level.

Mastering the Beginner Slope

Name: _____ **Age:** _____ **Date:** _____

Directions: Copy the Beginner Slope list from the "Building a Symptom Hierarchy" form. Start with the easiest symptom to resist and finish with the hardest. Below the list, you and the therapist should write down a plan to work on each problem. Sign it when you're done.

The Beginner Slope list
1.   Easier
2.
3.   Harder
others:
Working on problem 1: Steps:
Working on problem 2: Steps:
Working on problem 3: Steps:
Other problems: Steps:
WARNING: *In order to ski this slope, you must work on the problems that you listed on the Beginner Slope. Your next level is the Advanced Beginner Slope.*

_____   _____
Child's signature   **Therapist's signature**

Mastering the Advanced Beginner Slope

Name: _____ **Age:** _____ **Date:** _____

Directions: Copy the Advanced Beginner Slope list from the "Building a Symptom Hierarchy" form. Start with the easiest symptom to resist and finish with the hardest. Below the list, you and the therapist should write down a plan to work on each problem. Sign it when you're done.

The Advanced Beginner Slope list
1.   Easier
2.
3.   Harder
others:
Working on problem 1: Steps:
Working on problem 2: Steps:
Working on problem 3: Steps:
Other problems: Steps:
WARNING: *In order to ski this slope, you must work on the problems that are listed on the Advanced Beginner Slope. Your next level is the Intermediate Slope.*   _____   _____ **Child's signature**   **Therapist's signature**

Mastering the Intermediate Slope

Name: _____ **Age:** _____ **Date:** _____

Directions: Copy the Intermediate Slope list from the "Building a Symptom Hierarchy" form. Start with the easiest symptom to resist and finish with the hardest. Below the list, you and the therapist must write down a plan to work on each problem. Sign it when you're done.

The Intermediate Slope list
1.   Easier
2.
3.   Harder
others:
Working on problem 1: Steps:
Working on problem 2: Steps:
Working on problem 3: Steps:
Other problems: Steps:
WARNING: *In order to ski this slope, you must work on the problems that you listed on the Intermediate Slope. Your next level is the Advanced Intermediate Slope.*
_____   _____ **Child's signature**   **Therapist's signature**

Mastering the Advanced Intermediate Slope

Name: _____ **Age:** _____ **Date:** _____

Directions: Copy the Advanced Intermediate Slope list from the "Building a Symptom Hierarchy" form. Start with the easiest symptom to resist and finish with the hardest. Below the list, you and the therapist should write down a plan to work on each problem. Sign it when you're done.

The Advanced Intermediate Slope list
1.   Easier
2.
3.   Harder
others:
Working on problem 1: Steps:
Working on problem 2: Steps:
Working on problem 3: Steps:
Other problems: Steps:
WARNING: *In order to ski this slope, you must work on the problems that you listed on the Advanced Intermediate Slope. YOU ARE DOING GREAT! YOUR NEXT LEVEL IS THE EXPERT SLOPE!*

_____   _____

Child's signature   **Therapist's signature**

Mastering the Expert Slope

Name: _____ **Age:** _____ **Date:** _____

Directions: Copy the Expert Slope list from the "Building a Symptom Hierarchy" form. Start with the easiest symptom to resist and finish with the hardest. Below the list, you and the therapist should write down a plan to work on each problem. Sign it when you're done.

The Expert Slope list
1.   Easier
2.
3.   Harder
others:
Working on problem 1:   Steps:
Working on problem 2:   Steps:
Working on problem 3:   Steps:
Other problems: Steps:
Congratulations! *You have already mastered the Advanced Intermediate Slope. The Expert Slope is the hardest of all rides. DON'T GIVE UP! YOU CAN MAKE IT!*
_____   _____   **Child's signature**   **Therapist's signature**

The Skier's Chart

Directions: Each week put an X at the ski level you have achieved.

	SKIER'S LEVEL				
	Level 1	Level 2	Level 3	Level 4	Level 5
Week 1					
Week 2					
Week 3					
Week 4					
Week 5					
Week 6					
Week 7					
Week 8					
Week 9					
Week 10					
Week 11					
Week 12					
Week 13					
Week 14					
Week 15					

Key

Level 1 = Beginner Slope

Level 2 = Advanced Beginner Slope

Level 3 = Intermediate Slope

Level 4 = Advanced Intermediate Slope

Level 5 = Expert Slope

Differentiating the Child and the OCD

It is not uncommon for OCD to become the main focus of children's lives. Other aspects of their lives receive less and less attention from parents and others. The "Differentiating the Child and the OCD" form was designed to help children understand that even though they have OCD and it is a part of their lives, they are much more than the problem. It reminds children of positive aspects about themselves that can help them fight their disorder. It may also decrease secondary emotions such as depression and anger and may increase their motivation to get better. Separating children from the illness is an important part of the treatment.

Differentiating the Child and the OCD

Name: _____ **Age:** _____ **Date:** _____

Directions: Fill out each square. At the bottom of this form, complete the sentences.

NOTE: You may help the child generate ideas. If needed, parents may also help.

ME	OCD
Describe how you look.	Describe how you imagine the OCD to look.
Name five things that you like to do.	Name five things that the OCD likes to do.
Name a few things that you are good at.	Name a few things that the OCD is good at.

Complete these sentences about yourself:

My name is_____.

My favorite color is_____.

The last movie I watched was_____.

My favorite pet is _____.

I am good at_____.

A Picture of the Child

Name: _____ **Age:** _____ **Date:** _____

Directions: Draw yourself doing one or more things that you like to do.

A Picture of the OCD

Name: _____ **Age:** _____ **Date:** _____

Directions: Draw the OCD the way you imagine it to look.

NOTE: If the child has difficulty drawing the OCD, suggest drawing how the OCD makes him or her feel (e.g. scared, anxious, sad, etc.)

OCD and Non-OCD Thoughts

Learning how to differentiate between OCD thoughts and non OCD thoughts are an important part of the education portion of the treatment. Even though every child has different symptoms, the thoughts and behavioral patterns that each displays are similar. This list of different possible thoughts may help the child identify some of his or her OCD symptoms. Knowing about the symptoms may help the child recognize them when they are just beginning.

Learning about OCD symptoms that the child has not experienced may also be helpful. It may be easier for the child to recognize in other people's symptoms the unrealistic aspects of OCD thoughts and the senselessness of the compulsions. This may, in turn, help the child to understand his or her own symptoms.

OCD and Non-OCD Thoughts

Name: _____ **Age:** _____ **Date:** _____

Directions: In every cloud you will find a thought. Some will be OCD thoughts and some will just be normal, everyday thoughts that are not OCD. Circle the thoughts that you think could be from the OCD:

I have to wash my hands till they feel really clean.

I must blink before I get into the bus, so the bus will not crash.

I always want to take a shower before I go to a birthday party.

I love ice cream with hot fudge sauce.

I love my mom, even when I am not with her.

I worry about my mom and dad and hope that nothing bad happens to them.

I can't pet my dog because I may get sick.

I have to clear my mind every time I think a bad thought.

I like taking pictures of my family.

I have to make things line up perfectly.

In school, I like to go to the bathroom during recess.

Sometimes I have nightmares and I get scared.

I can't go to the bathroom in school, because I'm afraid of the germs.

If I scratch one side of my face, I have to scratch the other to make it even.

I have to do some habits so nothing bad happens to my parents.

I would like to collect stickers and place them in my book.

I have to tell my mom that I love her five times and then kiss her twice.

My Thoughts Worksheet

Directions: Make three clouds with OCD thoughts and three with normal everyday thoughts (Try to write down your own thoughts. If you like, make more clouds to fit more thoughts.) After you finish, test your therapist by asking him or her to put an X through the thoughts that are OCD.

OCD Location Chart

The "OCD Location Chart" form may help children understand how OCD impacts their life and why it is important to target specific symptoms for treatment. It is not uncommon for OCD to manifest itself differently in different situations. Sometimes children may function well in school, but when they come home they have a large number of rituals they have to perform. As symptoms worsen, children often have more difficulty controlling their urges, and their symptoms become more evident and more public. It is also common for symptoms to be suppressed in a strange setting or around someone that the child does not know well. As the child becomes more familiar with the situation, symptoms tend to reappear.

OCD Location Chart

Name: _____ **Age:** _____ **Date:** _____

Directions: In each square, write down OCD things that you think can bother kids (including yourself) when they are in the following places:

The Classroom	The Bathroom

The Bedroom	Outside (Public Places)

Write down other places and situations where the OCD bothers you:

1. ....

2. ....

3. ....

Directions: Put an X next to those situations that do not provoke OCD symptoms:

___ in school	___ when I meet a new person	___ at a party
___ at my friend's house	___ when I am in a new place	___ during recess
___ around my family	___ when I am alone	___ in front of friends

45

Giving In to the OCD

Children suffering from OCD usually experience some symptoms that are easy to fight and others that are harder. The "Me and The O.C. Flea" form will help the child identify situations where he or she is not able to resist engaging in the symptom. It also allows the therapist to assess the cognition that may lead to compulsions and helps the child identify thoughts that may trigger their symptoms.

NOTE: In the forms "Giving In to the OCD", p. 47, "Feelings and Consequences of Not Resisting the Symptoms", p. 49, "Not Giving In to OCD", p. 51, and "Feelings and Consequences of Resisting the Symptoms", p. 53, the OCD is referred to as the O.C. Flea. The O.C. Flea in this form is the messenger that brings the OCD messages to the child. O.C. Flea is also a character in *Blink, Blink, Clop, Clop, Why Do We Do Things We Can't Stop: An OCD Storybook*.

Giving In to the OCD

Name: _____ **Age:** _____ **Date:** _____

Directions: Draw yourself and create a conversation between the you and O.C. Flea.
In this conversation O.C. Flea tricks you into doing the habits and/or having the thoughts.

Child:	O.C. Flea:

Feelings and Consequences of Not Resisting the Symptoms

Based on the dialogue created in "Giving In to the OCD" the therapist uses the form "Feelings and Consequences of Not Resisting the Symptoms" to address the feelings and consequences of following O.C. Flea's messages. With this form, you can help children understand that when they engage in the symptom, they might feel better right after, but later they will feel anxious and compelled to do the behaviors again.

Feelings and Consequences of Not Resisting the Symptoms

Name: _____ **Age:** _____ **Date:** _____

Directions: Draw what you look like when you first do what the O.C. Flea tells you to do.
Then draw what you look like later on, when you feel nervous again and have to do more habits.
Finally, complete the sentences below the pictures.

Right after...	Later on...
When I do what O.C. Flea tells me,	But later on, I

Directions: Pick the feeling or feelings that match the situation, write them in the box then
draw the faces.

O.C. Flea tells me what to do

I do what O.C. Flea told me

O.C. Flea makes me do it again later

Sad	Happy	Disappointed	Silly
Nervous	Tired	Scared	Shy
Relieved	Bored	Proud	Grouchy
Frustrated	Angry	Surprised	Curious

Not Giving In to the OCD

This form allows the child to create a situation where he or she is able to resist engaging in compulsions and avoidance. It also gives the therapist an opportunity to positively reinforce the effort of trying to resist the symptoms and can also help the child to practice self-coping statements to fight urges and symptoms.

NOTE: Comparing the feelings from "Giving In to the OCD", p. 47, and "Not Giving In to the OCD" may help the child understand the long-term benefits of not following O.C. Flea's messages.

Not Giving In to the OCD

Name: _____ **Age:** _____ **Date:** _____

Directions: Draw yourself and create a conversation between the you and O.C. Flea. In this conversation O.C. Flea tries to trick you into doing the habits and/or having the thoughts, but you tell the O.C. Flea Off!

| Child: | O.C. Flea: |

Feelings and Consequences of Resisting the Symptoms

Based on the dialogue created in "Not Giving In to the OCD", p 51, the therapist uses this form to address the feelings and consequences of not following O.C. Flea's messages. With this form, you can help the child to understand that anxiety will be experienced at first when he or she does not engage in the symptom. However, the anxiety will eventually decrease and the urges of doing the OCD behaviors will also lessen.

Feelings and Consequences of Resisting the Symptoms

Name: _____ **Age:** _____ **Date:** _____

Directions: Draw what you look like when you don't do what the O.C. Flea tells you to do. Then draw what you look like you later on, when you feel better and have to do less habits. Finally, complete the sentences below the pictures.

Right after...	Later on...
When I don't do what O.C. Flea tells me,	But later on, I

Directions: Pick the feeling or feelings that match the situation, write them in the box, and draw the faces.

O.C. Flea tells me what to do

I DON'T DO IT !!

Later, I don't have to do it AGAIN!!

Sad	Happy	Disappointed	Silly
Nervous	Tired	Scared	Shy
Relief	Bored	Proud	Grouchy
Frustrated	Angry	Surprised	Curious

What Parents Can Do to Help

Parent participation in the behavioral treatment is usually necessary. Their understanding about the illness and knowledge about what will help their child may increase the likelihood of a positive treatment outcome. The "What Parents Can Do to Help" form lists some of the ways parents can contribute to alleviating their child's OCD symptoms.

What Parents Can Do to Help

Educate themselves: Parents should learn as much as possible about the symptoms, the most up-to-date treatment modalities, and the exposure and response prevention treatments. Parents should also work closely with the child's doctor or therapist, and learn about the pros and cons of using medication.

Ask questions: It is not simple to deal with a child suffering from OCD. Using common sense may not always help. Parents need to ask the child's therapist or doctor about how to deal with specific issues.

Focus: Parents should try to redirect their focus from the OCD symptoms to the child's positive behaviors.

Look for positives: Parents need to reinforce positive aspects of their child's behavior and personality (e.g., being a good sibling, a good reader, a good player, etc.)

Positive self-talk: When seeing their child struggle with a symptom parents should encourage the child to talk to him or herself using reasoning and positive thinking. It may help the child to not give in to the symptom so easily.

Humor can help: Parents should use humor to help their child fight the OCD symptoms, but not make fun of the child or the symptom. Making the situation seem "light" and not impossible to overcome is recommended.

Child versus the OCD: Parents should learn how to differentiate their child's normal behaviors from OCD symptoms and remember that children suffering from OCD are still children.

Healthy practices: Parents should get their child involved in normal "fun" activities, such as going to the movies, playing sports, and eating out. These activities may serve as natural exposure and therefore help your child.

Predictions: By now you must have some idea how OCD impacts your and your child's life. Parents need to predict situations that may be a problem and work with the child's therapist in finding more positive ways to handle them. Parents should try not to avoid these situations; instead, use them to help their child improve.

Support from others: Parents need to develop a strong support system. Support groups, as well as other parents of children with OCD, may be of great help to parents and their families.

Over-involvement: Parents must avoid getting involved with their child's symptoms. It is not helpful for the parent, the child, or the treatment.

Maintain your life: OCD may come to run the family's household as well as their lives. Parents must try not to stop living because of their child's illness. It is important for parents to keep things in perspective. The more normal the home environment is, the easier it will be for their child.

Hope: Parents must try to be realistic about their child's condition. However, this does not mean to give up hope. Parents should help their child by believing that he or she can, and will, get better. Dealing with OCD is a great challenge; your child needs your support and encouragement. The child's belief that he or she can fight this illness is very important for recovery.

What Is *Not* Helpful to the Child

In many situations common sense does not help parents deal with their child's symptoms. For example, parents believe that by answering their child's reassurance-seeking questions, they are helping the child not to worry. Research and clinical experience show that the opposite is true; the more parents answer the reassurance-seeking questions, the more doubt the child experiences and the more questions he or she asks. The "What Is *Not* Helpful to the Child" form lists some of the common mistakes parents make when dealing with the symptoms of childhood OCD.

What Is *Not* Helpful to the Child

Punishment: Parent should not punish their children for their OCD behaviors. Punishment will not help the symptoms decrease. Dealing with OCD sometimes feels like a punishment in itself. Nobody is to blame for this problem. Parents must be reminded that as hard as it is for them, they must try to imagine how their child may be feeling.

Physical violence: Even though watching their child's symptoms can be very frustrating, parents must never use violence or attempt to restrain their child from engaging in compulsions. It will negatively impact their child's symptoms, treatment, and the relationship with him or her.

"Helping out": It is very normal for parents to feel bad because their child spends so much time doing the OCD behaviors. Parents may feel an "urge" to help their child with the behaviors. Many parents think it will make things go smoother and be less painful for everybody. This may seem to be true for a few seconds. But in fact it will makes things worse. Parents must learn that helping their child do the OCD behaviors will reinforce the symptoms, possibly making them even stronger.

Answering all the questions: Many parents feel that it is their responsibility to answer all their child's questions and concerns. However, one very common symptom in children suffering from OCD is for them to ask for constant reassurance. Parents should talk to their child's therapist to help them differentiate between normal "curiosity" and an OCD symptom called *reassurance-seeking behavior*. The more parents answer these kinds of questions, the more doubt children with OCD experience. The child's therapist should be able to help parents learn how <u>not</u> to give reassurance.

Your child is not the OCD: Parents must understand that their child suffers from OCD; he or she is not the OCD. Making that differentiation may help parents sort their feelings.

Feeling angry: When parents feel angry and frustrated because their child's OCD made them late for an appointment, they should try to remember that it is the symptoms that they should be angry at, not the child. It is important for the child to understand that parents are not angry with him or her, but that nobody is happy with the OCD.

Shame: Some OCD symptoms can be very strange. It is not uncommon for parents to feel embarrassed when these symptoms are displayed in public. Parents should not let the shame become the most important aspect of their child's illness. Parents must remember that their child's urges to perform the behaviors must be very strong. Helping their child to get better should be the most important thing.

Parent Quiz

Many parents have a good understanding about OCD and the behavioral treatment. However, they experience difficulties with the everyday situations they encounter. The "Parent Quiz" gives parents an opportunity to think about issues related to the OCD symptoms. The therapist can use this form to educate parents about different alternatives in dealing with specific situations.

Parent Quiz

Child's Name: _____   **Child's Age:** _____   **Date:** _____

Filled out by : _____

Directions: Answer the following questions.

1. If my child wants me to watch him or her doing OCD behaviors, I should:

2. I should not buy extra soap because my child needs to wash his or her hands a lot:
   Yes _____ No _____   Why?

3. I should punish my child every time he or she does an OCD behavior:
   Yes _____ No _____   Why?

4. When I see my child having a hard time with the OCD, I should:

5. I should not help my child do OCD behaviors so that he or she will go to bed faster or get to the bus, because:

6. Fighting the OCD is very hard. Therefore, I should treat my child differently and let him or her do anything.
   Yes _____ No _____   Why?

7. I will make an effort to bring positive experiences into my child's life. This way, my child will realize he or she can be happy despite the OCD.
I could:

8. I should talk about OCD with my child.
Yes _____ No_____   Why?

9. I should talk about OCD all the time with my child.
Yes _____ No_____   Why?

10. What should I do when the treatment program is over?

How Parents Picture the OCD

It may be hard for children to understand how their parents feel about their OCD. It is not uncommon for children to believe that their parents are angry with them because they have this disorder. The form "How Parents Picture the OCD" gives parents an opportunity to envision the problem and can also help the child to see how his or her parents view the disorder.

How Parents Picture the OCD

Child's Name: _____   **Age:** _____   **Date:** _____

Filled out by: _____

Directions (to parents): Draw a picture of what the OCD represents to you.

Directions (to parents): Write a short paragraph or story about what OCD means to you and how it makes you feel.

NOTE: This activity may help your child better understand how you perceive his or her symptoms.

Showers Worksheet

Very often children with OCD have problems with showering. They may shower many times and/or for long periods of time. They may avoid showering altogether because it becomes too hard. Showering may be a problem because of contamination fears (germs or dirt), dressing and undressing compulsions, repetitiveness, and so on. The "Showers Worksheet" was designed to assess specific aspects of showering, and the information gained can be incorporated into the behavioral program. For example, following a strict routine when showering should be considered a target for treatment. This form can be used to collect baseline information and can also be used as a post-treatment measure.

Showers Worksheet

Name: _____ **Age:** _____ **Date:** _____

Directions: Take this form home. With your parents' help, fill out the chart below for one week. In the first row of the chart put the days of the week. Start with the day of your session (i.e. if your session is on Monday, the first date in the chart is Monday).

Day of Week							
Number of showers							
Length of							
Showers							

List of items used for hygiene (soap, etc.):

Now list your body parts in the order that you wash them.

Order of washing:

1.

2.

3.

4.

5.

Finally, answer the following questions:

Do you wash your hands before you start the shower?	**Yes**	**No**
Do you wash your hands during the shower?	**Yes**	**No**
I wash my hands after washing my:		
I wash my hands before washing my:		
One part of my body I cannot wash is:		
Do your parents help you take a shower?	**Yes**	**No**
Do you have to wear anything on your hands when you shower? If yes, what?	**Yes**	**No**

The Hand Wash Count

Hand washing is one of the most common symptoms of childhood OCD. Children experiencing hand-washing compulsions may have difficulty estimating how many times they wash their hands or how much soap they use. To create a progressive response prevention plan for these behaviors, use this form to collect baseline information and measure subsequent progress in hand-washing behaviors.

The Hand Wash Count

Name: _____ **Age:** _____ **Date:** _____

Directions: Every time you wash your hands make a small circle (a bubble) in that day's square:

Today is: _____	Today is: _____
Today is: _____	Today is: _____
Today is: _____	Today is: _____
Today is: _____	This week I washed a lot when I... 1. _____ 2. _____ 3. _____ 4. _____ 5. _____

Count your bubbles and write down the total number for each day.

Monday	Tuesday	Wednesday	Thursday	Friday	Saturday	Sunday

Counting Behaviors

Repetitive behaviors such as hand washing, motor body movements, and saying or thinking specific words are common symptoms of OCD. Counting these behaviors can be very helpful. In order to decrease the frequency of a symptom, it is necessary to know how often it occurs. (Increasing the child's awareness of the behavior can, in and of itself, help the child decrease some behaviors.) A counter will pick up even small changes in the occurrence of the behavior, which can allow the therapist to immediately reinforce the improved behavior.

Counting Behaviors

Name: _____ **Age:** _____ **Date:** _____

Directions: Obtain a portable hand-counter (available in most office-supply stores). Write down the behavior to be counted. Carry the counter in your pocket, and press the button every time the behavior occurs. At the end of the day, write down the number indicated by the counter on the chart below.

NOTE: If counting hand washings, ask the child if he or she perceives the counter as contaminated. You may also ask the child to press the counter's button prior to him or her washing hands.

Behavior	Mon.	Tues.	Wed.	Thurs.	Fri.	Sat.	Sun.
Week 1							
Week 2							
Week 3							
Week 4							
Week 5							
Week 6							
Week 7							
Week 8							
Week 9							
Week 10							
Week 11							
Week 12							
Week 13							
Week 14							
Week 15							

Avoided Objects Chart

This form can be very helpful to therapists who use exposure exercises in treating childhood OCD. Exposure exercises can be an important behavioral therapy for OCD. However, its use is controversial due to the child's increased anxiety levels. When doing exposure exercises with children, try to make it as much fun as possible. Also, the child must agree to any increase in the difficulty level of the exercises. This form should help the child identify the objects that they have difficulty touching (due to contamination fears or for other reasons).

Avoided Objects Chart

Name: _____ **Date:** _____

Directions: If possible, paste the actual items that you have a hard time touching on the chart below. If you can't put the actual item on the chart, you may rub a tissue on it and paste that on the "Untouchable" board. Name the items in each spot.

The Untouchable Board	
Paste the item here	*Paste the item here*
This is	This is
Paste the item here	*Paste the item here*
This is	This is

Exposure and Avoidance Point Chart

There are many important components to be aware of when implementing exposure exercises. To a child with OCD, different objects or situations involve varying degrees of contamination. For example, a bathroom at home may seem less contaminated than a public bathroom. Another aspect of contamination fears is the closeness of the contaminate to the child's "protected" areas. Many times having the contaminate touch the face, hair, or bed will increase the child's anxiety more than if he or she had to touch the object lightly with a hand.

The behaviors that take place after the exposure exercise are also very important. For example, children may be able to touch the contaminate but then will wash their hands until they feel clean again. When the exposure exercise involves contamination, the goal is to experience increasing contamination and be less and less concerned about "being clean." In the "Exposure and Avoidance Point Chart," children receive more points as they complete harder exposure combined with less washing.

NOTE: The therapist must adjust the points given according to the child's symptom severity. For example, not washing hands at all or washing without soap may be seen as impossible for some children if their symptoms are severe.

Exposure and Avoidance Point Chart

Name: _____   **Date:** _____

Directions: Practice touching the "untouchable" items from the chart with your therapist and at home. Check off the appropriate box that corresponds to each touching exercise. The more difficult the touch, the more points you will get. At the end of each week add the points you earned on the board (i.e., touched floor for few seconds (2 points) + wash with no soap (4 points) = 6 points).

Item	no wash 5	wash/no soap 4	wash/ little soap 3	wash 1x w/soap 2	wash 2 x or more decrease=1 same=0 ( )
light 1					
few seconds 2					
hair & face 3					
rub & hold 4					
carry it on you 5					
place in your bed 6					
total points (touch + wash)					

Exposure and Avoidance Point Chart *(continued)*

Reward	Total of Points
Week one	
Week two	
Week three	
Week four	
Week five	
Week six	

Suggestions for rewards during the session:	Point Value
Verbal praises	
Smiles	
Stickers	
Playing a game	
Telling a funny story	
Drawing	
Using the computer	
Parents may bring soda or fun food	
Going out of the office with the child and parent	

Disclosing Obsessive Thoughts and Compulsive Behaviors

Talking about obsessive thoughts is a delicate issue in the treatment of children. Very often children refuse to talk about the thoughts they are experiencing. They may be embarrassed or afraid of being thought of as weird. Talking about their obsessive thoughts is a first step to desensitizing the feelings the thoughts invoke.

NOTE: Children may try to hide their rituals. Parents and therapists may not notice the bedtime rituals or mental compulsions because they are so easy for the child to hide. However, it is important that these symptoms be targeted and treated.

Disclosing Obsessive Thoughts and Compulsive Behaviors

Name: _____   **Age:** _____   **Date:** _____

Directions: Write down a thought and/or habit that you don't like talking about.

I don't like talking about this one, but I will write it here:

This one is the hardest one. I will write it, but I need to cover it. Eventually I will open it so that it can stop bothering me.

Now cut this piece of paper and tape it to the second box.

Do not open until I show you.

Perfectionism

Children with OCD tend to be perfectionists. Their perfectionism often affects their schoolwork and their ability to enjoy different activities. The "Writing with my Other Hand", p. 79, and "My Masterpiece", p. 80, forms help the child practice being imperfect. By trying to do things perfectly, perfectionists are often unable to finish their classwork, homework, and sometimes even standardized tests at school. The fear of feeling embarrassed or being judged by others may reinforce the need for perfection. Encourage the child to show these completed forms to other people.

Writing with my Other Hand

Directions: First write your name as you normally write it. Then write your name with your other hand. Finally, write your name with your eyes closed.

Name:
Name:
Name:
Now fold this piece of paper so that the first line with your name on it can't be seen. Show the other two to five people without telling them that you wrote them with your other hand and then with your eyes closed.
How many people were able to read your name?
How many people were not able to read your name?
Finally write your first and last name with your eyes closed and with the hand that you do not usually write with.
Name:

My Masterpiece

Directions: Draw something that you like and know how to draw well. Instead of trying to make it nice and perfect, make it look crooked and imperfect. Show to other people and tell them that this is your "masterpiece."

By_____

"What If" Questions

OCD children often display "what if" type thinking and reassurance-seeking behaviors. They ask questions over and over again. This chart was designed to help parents avoid reassuring their child. When parents stop the reassurances, the child usually reacts at first by asking even more questions. However, this behavior tends to decrease over time, and the reassurance-seeking behaviors may eventually be significantly reduced or extinguished.

Doubting is a common symptom of OCD. Many times children with OCD respond with an "I don't know" to questions that they do know the answers to. This chart will help to increase the child's awareness of these symptoms and monitor their occurrence.

"What If" Questions: Form #1

Name: _____   **Age:** _____   **Date:** _____

Directions (to the therapist):

1. Have the parents collect baseline data by counting the number of "what if" questions each day for a few days (between the current session and the next one). Use an average number per day as the baseline.

2. In the session, have the child and parents work together using the data from Form #1 to set the goals and small rewards (treats) for each day on Form #2. The goal should be to ask fewer "what if" questions each day.

3. Set a realistic goal for 1 week and a bigger reward if the goal achieved by the end of the week.

Put one mark down for every "what if" question	Total
Day 1	=
Day 2	=
Day 3	=
Day 4	=
Day 5	=
Day 6	=
Day 7	=
Average number of "what if" questions per day	=

"What If" Questions: Form #2

Directions: Over the course of a week mark down every time your child asks a "what if" type question. Add up the marks each day and write down the total. If the number on the total is equal or lower than the "goal," the child receives the "treat" for that specific day. After one week, if the child achieves the goal of the week, the child receives a reward.

NOTE: The goals, treats and rewards are agreed to in the prior session.

Day	Goal	"What if" questions	Total	Treat
Mon			=	
Tue			=	
Wed			=	
Thurs			=	
Fri			=	
Sat			=	
Sun			=	
		Goal after 1 week =		
The goal achieved	YES	Reward =		
Still working on it	YES	Incentive=		
Not even trying	YES	Sorry, start again		

Reassurance-Seeking Behaviors Chart

Reassurance-seeking behavior is a common symptom of OCD. The types of questions children ask parents vary according to a child's symptoms. A child concerned about getting sick may ask repetitive questions concerning health. Another child may ask questions about the time, the weather, or if he or she performed a certain behavior the right way.

Parents and other people surrounding the child may play an important role in the maintenance of this symptom. Often the child finds someone who will answer the questions over and over again, creating a cycle of more doubting and then more reassurance-seeking questions. The "Reassurance-Seeking Behaviors Chart" helps establish the frequency of this behavior. It can also help the child and the family understand that the more reassurance given to the child, the more the behavior will repeat itself.

Reassurance-Seeking Behaviors Chart

Name: _____ **Age:** _____ **Date:** _____

Directions (for parents): After each letter below, write down the most commonly asked questions by your child when seeking reassurance. In the first part of the chart place a mark under the letter that corresponds to the question asked that day. In the second part of the chart place a mark under the letter that corresponds to the question you answered that day.

A_____ **C**_____

B_____ **D**_____

(Mark here every time the child asks the question)

	A	B	C	D	Total
Monday					
Tuesday					
Wednesday					
Thursday					
Friday					
Saturday					
Sunday					

(Mark here every time you answer the question)

	A	B	C	D	Total
Monday					
Tuesday					
Wednesday					
Thursday					
Friday					
Saturday					
Sunday					

Relapse Prevention Contract

The "Relapse Prevention Contract" form was designed to help the child feel more responsibility for the success of his or her treatment. The child will therefore become more involved with and committed to the behavioral program. This contract is also a reminder that fighting the OCD will help them get better.

Have the child complete the Relapse Prevention Contract in front of the parents. Parents or guardians can sign as witnesses.

Relapse Prevention Contract

I, _____, will continue to fight the following compulsions:
(Child's Name)

1. _____ 2. _____ 3. _____

I will not be afraid of the following OCD thoughts:

1. _____ 2. _____ 3. _____

Statement of Commitment:

I will not allow OCD to stop me from being a happy kid. I will do my best not to give in when I feel anxious or feel like I have to do the OCD stuff.

Please copy the following statement below:
I will fight the OCD every day so it will get smaller and smaller and stop bothering me.

_____

_____

I agree with all the above statements, and I will work to fulfill this contract.

_____   _____
(Child's signature)   **(date)**

_____   _____
(witness)   **(date)**

_____   _____
(therapist)   **(date)**

Diploma

The diploma for completion of treatment should be given in a "graduation ceremony." Have the child invite their parents and others to participate in this celebration.

CONGRATULATIONS

Champion Against OCD

_____ has completed a program of

control over OCD symptoms

on this day _____ of _____

in the year _____.

_____   _____
Therapist   **Parent**

Behavior Contingency Chart

Children suffering from OCD very often present other behavioral problems. It is important to separate OCD behaviors from other types of behaviors. The "Behavior Contingency Chart" can be used to record problem behaviors and their consequences. It can also help parents and teachers to be more consistent with enforcing consequences.

Behavior Contingency Chart

Child's Name: _____   **Age:** _____   **Date:** _____

Filled out by:_____

Directions: Write the information in each square.

Date/Time	Problem Behavior	Behavioral Outcome	Disciplinary Consequences	Child's Reaction

Reward Schedule

Positive behaviors as well as efforts to improve should be rewarded. Small rewards should be given before earning a bigger reward. The "Reward Schedule" form helps the child and family assign values to each reward. If a child receives the reward before exhibiting the positive behavior or does not receive the promised reward after the positive behavior, the behavior will not be reinforced.

Reward Schedule

Name: _____ **Age:** _____ **Date:** _____

Directions: Fill in the number of points needed to receive each of the following rewards.

	Points
A hug	
A kiss	
A cookie	
An extra half hour of television	
A special meal	
A trip to the zoo	
A cassette tape or a CD	
Extra time on the computer	
An ice cream cone	
A video rental	
Staying up a half hour later	
A story read to them	
Time alone with:	
Swimming	
Going to the movies	
A meal at a favorite restaurant	
Play sports with parents	
New crayons/markers	
A kid's magazine	
Extra time to play video games	
A small toy or prize	
Playing a game	

Feeling and Acting Chart

Children may be able to cope better if they practice reacting to different feelings and situations. The "Feeling and Acting Chart" addresses common feelings experienced by children with OCD and gives the child a chance to consider more positive ways to deal with negative situations and emotions.

Feeling and Acting Chart

Name: _____ **Age:** _____ **Date:** _____

Directions: Write down specific situations where you experienced the feelings listed below and then write positive ways to deal with those situations.

I felt frustrated	What I could have done
1.	
2.	
3.	
4.	

I felt embarrassed	What I could have done
1.	
2.	
3.	
4.	

I felt sad	What I could have done
1.	
2.	
3.	
4.	

I felt angry	What I could have done
1.	
2.	
3.	
4.	

I felt anxious	What I could have done
1.	
2.	
3.	
4.	

Home Chores Chart

In order to feel like part of the family, a child with OCD should be given responsibilities, just like the other members of the family. The more positive activities the child is motivated to engage in, the better it is for his or her overall functioning.

NOTE: Create the chart according to the child's abilities. If an OCD symptom interferes with the completion of a chore, pair the child with an adult to do that specific chore. The goal will be for the child to eventually do the chore on his or her own.

Home Chores Chart

Child's Name: _____ **Age:** _____ **Date:** _____

Filled out by: _____

Directions: With all the family members present, designate the week's chores to each child and adult. Write each person's name in the box followed by a description of the chore. Then put in the day and time for the chore to be performed. Make a check every time the chore is completed or a circle if the chore is not completed or is completed incorrectly.

	Mon.	Tues.	Wed.	Thurs.	Fri.	Sat.	Sun.
Name							
Chore							
Day & Time							
Name							
Chore							
Day & Time							
Name							
Chore							
Day & Time							
Name							
Chore							
Day & Time							
Name							
Chore							
Day & Time							
Name							
Chore							
Day & Time							

Homework Chart

Homework assignments are usually a source of stress for children with OCD. Because OCD symptoms are time consuming and may occur while children are doing their homework, finishing the homework in a reasonable amount of time is often impossible. To help children with homework problems, you may suggest having them keep track of how long it is taking to do the homework and set a time limit for its completion. The "Homework Chart" will help children organize their homework schedule and keep track of the amount of time allocated for this activity.

NOTE: Adding a reward schedule to this chart may help motivate the child to complete the homework assignments faster.

Homework Chart

Name: _____   **Week of:** _____

	Assignments	Starting Time/Ending Time
Monday		
Tuesday		
Wednesday		
Thursday		
Friday		

Achievement Certificate

Behavioral programs help children achieve goals and learn to follow rules set by the parent or therapist. Use the "Achievement Certificate" to reinforce and reward the child for mastering the targeted behaviors.

Congratulations to

_____

Who has mastered the following:

✔ ....

✔ ....

✔ ....

✔ ....

✔ ....

_____   _____

(Child's signature)   **(date)**

_____   _____

(Witness' signature)   **(date)**